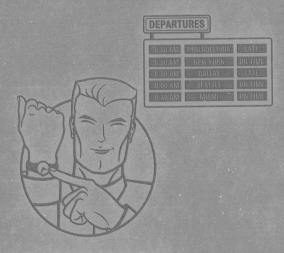

# COMMUTER
# WAITING GAMES

Library of Congress
Cataloging in Publication
Number 2002093883

ISBN: 1–931686–27–0

Manufactured in China

Designed by Paul Kepple @
Headcase Design

Illustrations by Timothy
Crawford @ Headcase Design

Distributed in
North America by
Chronicle Books
85 Second Street
San Francisco, CA 94105
10 9 8 7 6 5 4 3 2 1

Quirk Books
215 Church Street
Philadelphia, PA 19106
www.quirkbooks.com

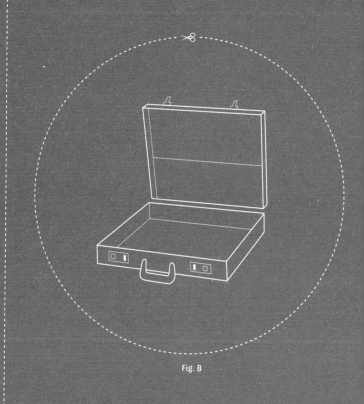

**Fig. B**

**Fig. C**

## ACKNOWLEDGMENTS

I'd like to thank all of the nine-to-fivers who worked overtime on this project,
particularly Timothy Crawford (who provided the terrific illustrations), Paul Kepple
(who provided the dazzling design), Emily Betsch (who designed the game on the cover),
Mindy Brown (who taught me the rules of Airport Check-in Limbo), Erin Slonaker (who
weeded out my typos), and the whole gang at Quirk Books. I'm also grateful to my
mentor, Jason Rekulak, who stages the best airplane puppet shows I've ever seen.

# COMMUTER WAITING GAMES

### Things to Do While Driving, Riding, or Flying

BY

## HAL BOWMAN

ILLUSTRATIONS BY TIMOTHY CRAWFORD

QUIRK

Fig. D

Fig. E

# C O N T E N T S

## IV: Biking and Walking Waiting Games

## V: Airplane Waiting Games

# INTRODUCING LLOYD

As the Official Spokesmodel of *Commuter Waiting Games*, veteran commuter Lloyd Hamilton will lead you through the activities in this book. With enough practice, you can acquire the skills that he demonstrates throughout these pages.

# INTRODUCTION

If you're a typical person living in the United States, you face a 25-minute commute to work every morning. And if you live to the average age of 74, you'll spend *more than one year of your life* traveling to and from your place of employment.

Maybe one year doesn't seem like much. After all, you'll spend eight years of your life eating meals. You'll spend another 13 years watching television.

But eating meals and watching TV are fun. Commuting is not. I recently completed a very scientific study via an e-mail to everyone in my office, and all three of the respondents agreed that commuting is the worst part of their day.

My own commute is particularly savage. To get to work, I spend 30 minutes in a car, another 40 minutes on a train, and then trek for 15 minutes on foot.

For years, I was miserable. I tried all of the usual morning commuter diversions. I listened to audio books by John Grisham and Mary Higgins Clark. I invested in a Palm Pilot and spent hours inputting my address book. I bought a cell phone and chatted for hours on adults-only 1-900 chat lines.

But I was still bored.

As the years passed, however, I gradually realized that you don't need laptops or Palm Pilots or Walkmans to enjoy your commute. In fact, these items actually *distract* you from the real pleasure of commuting—which is not *killing* time but *maximizing* your time and making the most of everything your commute has to offer. That means getting to know your fellow passengers. Using discarded newspapers, train seat checks, and airline blankets to create dazzling feats of art and architecture. Challenging other commuters to games of strategy and grueling athletic competitions.

The activities in this book will guide you through every kind of commuting situation imaginable, whether you're traveling by plane, train, automobile, elevator, bicycle, or good old-fashioned foot transport. You'll find instructions for making beautiful crafts, performing mind-bending magic tricks, playing carpool games, solving devious puzzles, and much more.

To demonstrate these activities, I've enlisted the help of a fellow commuter and co-worker, Lloyd Hamilton, who will serve as a spokesmodel throughout this book. Let his grace and poise be a model for your own endeavors.

And let's not waste any more time—off to work we go!

*Hal Bowman*

Hal Bowman
Paramus, New Jersey

# I

# TRAIN
## AND
# SUBWAY
## WAITING GAMES

I'm always astounded by people who do work on the train—after eight or more hours in the office, what drives them to continue crunching numbers, checking e-mails, and computing spreadsheets? It's bad enough that you have to crowd into a packed train with hundreds of other irritable commuters—you might as well enjoy the trip with the help of the following activities.

8 min.
or longer

DURATION

# DESIGN A NEWSPAPER BRIDAL GOWN

Every train has dozens of abandoned newspapers scattered around its seats—and it took a visionary like Martha Stewart to finally find a good use for them. Commuting legend and lore say that Stewart invented this contest one morning while traveling from Greenwich, Connecticut, to New York City on the Metro-North commuter railroad. I'm told that passengers on Metro-North honor Martha's legacy by partaking in these competitions on a regular basis.

## WHAT YOU'LL NEED:

Discarded newspapers

1. Players should divide into two teams of at least two players each. (Fig. A)

2. The newspapers should be distributed evenly between the two teams. (Fig. B)

3. Each team should designate a "Captain" and a "Bride." (Fig. C)

4. Using only newspaper (and no tape, glue, or string), teammates must dress the bride in the most beautiful wedding gown they can create.

5. Remember: Your bride's face is a portrait, and her neckline is the frame. Use long, two-inch strips of newspaper to construct the perfect neckline; tuck these strips under her collar or her bra straps. (Fig. D)

6. If your bride prefers to wear sleeves, wrap her upper arm and forearm separately, so she can still bend her arms at the elbows. (Fig. E)

7. You can add "lace" to the veil, train, or bodice by tearing the newspaper into tiny, frilly strips. (Fig. F)

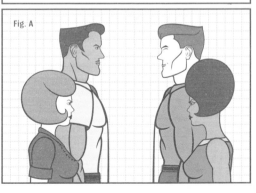

Fig. A

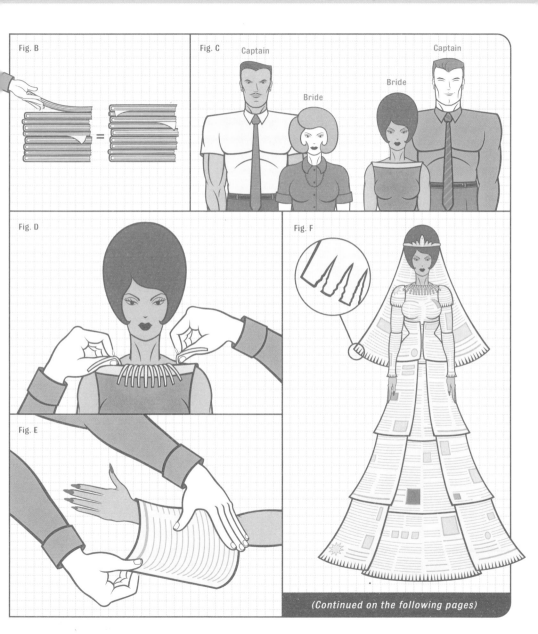

Fig. B

Fig. C
Captain
Bride
Bride
Captain

Fig. D

Fig. E

Fig. F

(Continued on the following pages)

**DESIGN A NEWSPAPER BRIDAL GOWN (continued)**

(8) When both brides are dressed, the captains must escort them down the aisle to the nearest conductor, who should pick the winning gown. (Fig. G)

(9) Afterward, all players should adjourn to the café car for a reception. Mazel tov!

Fig. G

# RUN A WATER CUP RELAY RACE

**3 min.** or less

DURATION

Have you ever been on a commuter train in the summer when the air-conditioning breaks down? It's not pleasant, let me tell you. And if you try to cool down by removing your shirt and socks, the conductors can be downright rude. You're better off trying this activity, which takes advantage of the water dispensers on Amtrak and other fancy commuter trains.

## WHAT YOU'LL NEED:

 Paper cups

 Water dispenser

 Goggles (optional)

1. Challenge the person sitting next to you to a water relay. (Fig. A)

2. Allow this person to select an unbiased referee. (Fig. B)

3. Each player should fill one cup all the way to the brim. (Fig. C)

4. The players should stand at opposite ends of the car. (Fig. D)

5. At the exact moment when the conductor announces the next stop, players should begin running toward the opposite ends of the car. (Fig. E)

6. Each player should "tag" the opposite door and run back to his original starting point. (Fig. F)

7. The first player to return to the starting point wins—unless the referee declares that his cup has less water in it than his opponent's. In that case, the opponent wins. (Fig. G)

Fig. A

Fig. B

Fig. C

Fig. D

Fig. E

Fig. F

Fig. G

8 min.
or longer

DURATION

# PLAY "NAME THAT TRAIN"

Public fascination with trains is reflected in every aspect of popular culture, from books and movies to pop music. But how much knowledge of pop culture do you and your fellow commuters really have? Play "Name That Train" to find out.

## WHAT YOU'LL NEED:

 Pencil

Paper

"Name That Train" is best played in a three-seater row, with a moderator in the middle and a contestant on either side.

(1) Based on the skill level and category, each player must bid how many clues he will need to solve the puzzle. Players may change bids based on the responses of other players (if you bid 3 but another commuter bids 2, you may re-bid 1). However, you may not bid any number that has already been claimed.

(2) The moderator reads the appropriate number of clues to the player with the lowest bid, starting with the first clue.

(3) If the player answers the question correctly, he receives the point value of his bid. If not, he receives a penalty of 10 points.

(4) The moderator should read all of the clues in the remaining player's bid. If this player

answers the question correctly, he receives the point value of his bid. If not, he also receives a 10-point penalty.

(5) If neither player answers correctly, the moderator should read the rest of the clues. The first person to answer correctly gets the point value of the last clue read; the other player receives a 10-point penalty.

(6) At the end of all six rounds, the player with the lowest score wins.

(See "Solutions," p. 84.)

SCORING:

| | |
|---|---|
| 19 or less: | Pick up your Amtrak job application immediately. Better yet, go audition for *Jeopardy!* |
| 20–35: | You must have studied engineering at some point. |
| 36–49: | It was that last TV question that screwed you up, wasn't it? |
| 50–60: | You're spending too much time at the office. Go home and watch TV! |

| Category: | Skill Level: |
|-----------|--------------|
| MUSIC | EASY |

(1) This song is based on a real-life train that embarked on its maiden journey in March of 1880.

(2) The train was a small wood-burning steam locomotive on the Cincinnati Southern Railroad.

(3) The song was featured in the film *Sun Valley Serenade*, where it was performed by Tex Beneke and the Modernaires.

(4) The music was written by Harry Warren; Mack Gordon takes credit for the lyrics.

(5) In the song, the train departs the Pennsylvania Station at 3:45.

(6) Or, more precisely, "a quarter to four."

(7) The singer boards the train on Track 29.

(8) He also enjoys a meal of ham and eggs in Carolina.

(9) The song was introduced by the Glenn Miller Orchestra in 1941.

(10) In the chorus, the singer asks the train, "Won't you choo-choo me home?"

| Category: | Skill Level: |
|-----------|--------------|
| LITERATURE | EASY |

(1) This book was written by Watty Piper in 1930.

(2) The train's cargo includes food and livestock.

(3) This book has full-color illustrations on every page.

(4) The engine is blue and "very little."

(5) The little blue engine was, in fact, a replacement for a little red engine that "could not go another inch."

(6) Among the train's passengers is Humpty Dumpty.

(7) Also on board are giraffes, elephants, toy soldiers, monkeys, and a yellow bear with a suspicious resemblance to Winnie the Pooh.

(8) At the book's climax, the train faces a huge mountain that appears impassable.

(9) Many other engines do not think they can climb it.

(10) But the little blue engine makes it to the top—all thanks to his mantra, "I think I can, I think I can."

*(Continued on the following pages)*

PLAY & NAME THAT TRAIN & (continued)

## Category: LITERATURE
## Skill Level: MEDIUM

1. This train began its maiden voyage on October 4, 1883.

2. It was the dream of Georges Nagelmackers, a Belgian railway enthusiast who also introduced the first restaurant car on a train.

3. Its initial route ran from Paris to Bucharest.

4. This real-life train was the subject of a popular 1934 mystery novel.

5. In the mystery, a wealthy American is found stabbed to death in the night compartment of the Calais coach.

6. The mystery's original title was *Murder in the Calais Coach*.

7. Suspects in the mystery include Hildegarde Schmidt, Countess Andrenyi, and Princess Dragomiroff.

8. The mystery was adapted into an Academy Award–winning 1974 film starring Albert Finney.

9. In the film, Finney played detective mastermind Hercule Poirot.

10. The novel's author, Dame Agatha Christie, has more than two billion copies of her books in print.

## Category: MOVIES
## Skill Level: MEDIUM

1. Among this train's passengers is Patrick McGoohan, aka #6 on *The Prisoner*.

2. Also on board are Fred Willard, Ned Beatty, and Scatman Crothers.

3. This train departs from Los Angeles and arrives nearly 72 hours later in Chicago.

4. The National Rail Passenger Corporation (now Amtrak) feared adverse publicity because of a gigantic crash at the end of the film. Consequently, the producers cut a deal with the Canadian Pacific Railway.

5. Posters called it "The Most Hilarious Suspense Ride of Your Life!"

6. The hero is a daffy book editor who thinks he sees a man thrown from the train.

7. His love interest was nominated for best actress for her role in *An Unmarried Woman*.

8. The film was released in 1976.

9. It starred Gene Wilder and Jill Clayburgh.

10. In the movie's most famous scene, Gene Wilder disguises himself in blackface and joins Richard Pryor in a hilarious walk through a train station in Chicago.

| Category: | Skill Level: |
|-----------|--------------|
| TELEVISION | DIFFICULT |

1. This train debuted on a local Chicago network in 1970.

2. One year later, it entered syndication in Atlanta, Cleveland, Detroit, Houston, Los Angeles, Philadelphia, and San Francisco.

3. Despite the show's increasing popularity, many cities initially refused to carry it.

4. These days, it's the longest-running program produced for first-run TV syndication.

5. President Clinton appeared at this show's 25th anniversary gala and claimed he had been "a fan for a long time."

6. The "conductor" of this train, Don Cornelius, was awarded a star on the Hollywood Walk of Fame.

7. In the '70s, this train's passenger list included guests Diana Ross, Bill Cosby, and Marvin Gaye.

8. More recent "passengers" have included Lil' Mo, Lil' Zane, and Lil' Bow Wow.

9. Every year, this train sponsors an annual live music awards special.

10. When it premiered, many called it an R&B version of *American Bandstand*.

| Category: | Skill Level: |
|-----------|--------------|
| TELEVISION | DIFFICULT |

1. The cast included Edward Andrews, Harry Flood, Patrick Collins, and Nita Talbot—in other words, people you've never heard of.

2. The series itself was produced by Dan Curtis, producer of *Dark Shadows*.

3. It was yanked after four episodes and turned over to Robert Stambler.

4. It lasted only five months—and was deemed by many a "super disaster."

5. In 1978, NBC exec Fred Silverman decided that TV viewers would enjoy a series very similar to *The Love Boat*—only set on a train.

6. And not just an ordinary train, but an atomic-powered train that could reach speeds of 200 miles an hour.

7. It could travel coast to coast in just 36 hours.

8. This amazing train was so large, it supposedly ran on two sets of parallel tracks.

9. At the time, the set was among the most expensive ever designed for television. The train included a disco, gymnasium, shopping center, and Olympic-sized swimming pool.

10. Look! Up in the sky! It's a bird! It's a plane! It's—

**8 min.**
or longer

DURATION

# WHAT'S WRONG WITH THIS TRAIN STATION?

It's 6:15 in the morning and Lloyd is getting ready to board his train—but hold on a second! Savvy commuters will recognize that there are at least ten mistakes in this drawing. How many can you find? (See "Solutions," p. 84.)

# PRACTICE TRAINSCENDENTAL MEDITATION

**8 min.**
or longer

DURATION

Although it might sound similar to Transcendental Meditation, the meditation techniques described here are actually much simpler (and perfect for the hectic environments of commuter trains and subways). Let Lloyd serve as your guide—but remember, there are no right or wrong ways to do this. Choose the method that works for you.

  ## WHAT YOU'LL NEED:

Newspapers

1. Collect some old newspapers from the train cabins and carry them to an open space. (Fig. A) The platform between cars is an excellent place to meditate, if the conductor will allow you to sit there.

2. Place the newspapers on the platform (or other open space) and sit cross-legged on the newspaper. (Fig. B)

3. Sit with pride and dignity. Your body should be relaxed. Notice how Lloyd rests his arms comfortably on his thighs. Your mouth may hang open slightly, and you may want to close your eyes. (Fig. C)

4. Begin to relax your mind: Pay attention to your breathing. Concentrate on your exhalations. Listen to the train passing over the rails. Let the soothing static of the PA system wash over you.

5. As thoughts enter your mind, simply label them as thoughts. There are no good thoughts or bad thoughts. Dismiss them, and concentrate on your breathing.

6. Experiment with the rhythm of your breathing. Do not worry about whether you are "doing it right." Do what feels best for you.

7. Hold your train pass in your right hand, so that you will not be interrupted when the conductor approaches you. (Fig. D)

As you begin, five or ten minutes of meditation will be more than enough. But with daily practice, you can work yourself up to sessions of 30 minutes or even longer. In time, you will even stop taking express trains, because they don't offer enough time for you to concentrate.

Fig. A

Fig. B

Fig. C

Fig. D

# WIN FREE DRINKS IN THE CAFÉ CAR

less than
**3 min.**

D U R A T I O N

Many a commuter has decided that the best way to spend a train ride is to be intoxicated—which would be fine, in my opinion, if the drinks weren't so ridiculously overpriced. But by striking up conversations with unsuspecting marks, you can use this incredible math trick to win all the free drinks you want. To demonstrate scientific credibility, punch the numbers into your Palm Pilot calculator.

## WHAT YOU'LL NEED:

 Palm Pilot

(1) While waiting in line at the café car, tell the person ahead of you that you can predict his phone number and age if he just does a few math problems on your Palm Pilot.

(2) When this person expresses disbelief, offer to make a wager: If you can do it, he has to buy the first round. If not, you'll pay his train fare.

(3) Hand over your Palm Pilot, and ask your mark to enter his seven-digit phone number (no area code) into the calculator.

(4) Have him multiply the results by 2 . . .

(5) then add 5 . . .

(6) and multiply the results by 50 . . .

(7) and then add his age . . .

(8) and add the number of days in an average year.

(9) For the last step, I like to add a little dramatic flourish. Sometimes I'll say, "This is the 6:15 train, isn't it?" Or I'll point out that a drink plus tax will probably cost six dollars and fifteen cents. Whatever your technique, you must ask your mark to subtract 615 from the total.

(10) The number in the display will be your mark's phone number and age. For example, if the display reads 875991330, his phone number is 875-9913, and his age is 30.

# DO TRAIN AND SUBWAY CALISTHENICS

**8 min.**
or longer

DURATION

Maybe it's my imagination, but sometimes I'll be sitting on a commuter train or subway and I can feel my body growing fatter. This feeling is exacerbated whenever there's a delay in traffic; once, after idling for 20 minutes at a station platform, I ran off the train, burst into the closest gym, and signed up for a three-year membership. Before you make the same mistake, try burning calories and frustration with these tried-and-true calisthenic exercises.

 **WHAT YOU'LL NEED:**

Leotard (optional)

## TRAIN AISLE DIPS
*Skill Level: Easy*

1. Stand in the aisle and grasp the tops of the seats on your left and your right. (Fig. A) If the seats have special straps for holding seat checks in place, wedge your hands underneath these straps.

*(Continued on the following pages)*

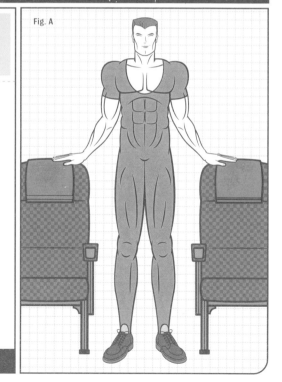

Fig. A

(2) Push yourself up in the air. Notice how Lloyd keeps his knees bent and his ankles crossed. (Fig. B)

(3) Lower yourself until your knees are a few inches from the floor. (Fig. C)

(4) Then lift yourself up again. (Fig. D)

(5) Repeat 12 times. (Fig. E)

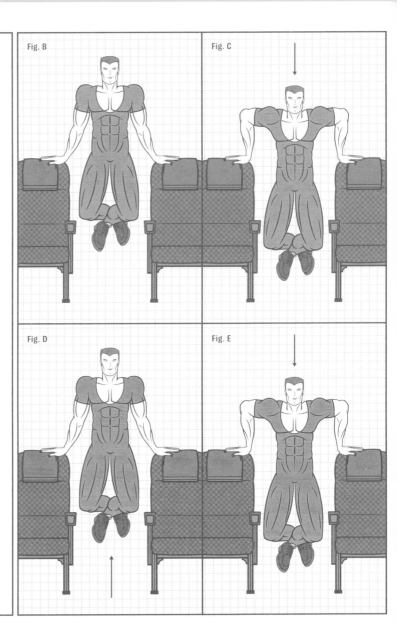

Fig. B

Fig. C

Fig. D

Fig. E

# SUBWAY HANDLE PULL-UPS

*Skill Level: Medium*

1. Stand in front of your seat, face the window, and grasp the overhead handles, placing your hands as far apart as possible. (Fig. A)

2. Hang from the handles with your knees bent and your ankles slightly crossed. (Fig. B)

3. Slowly pull yourself up until your chin is over the handles. (Fig. C)

4. Hold for a moment, then return to starting position.

5. Repeat without resting for 12 repetitions.

6. Don't be shy about asking your fellow commuters to hold your legs and give you an extra boost. (Fig. D)

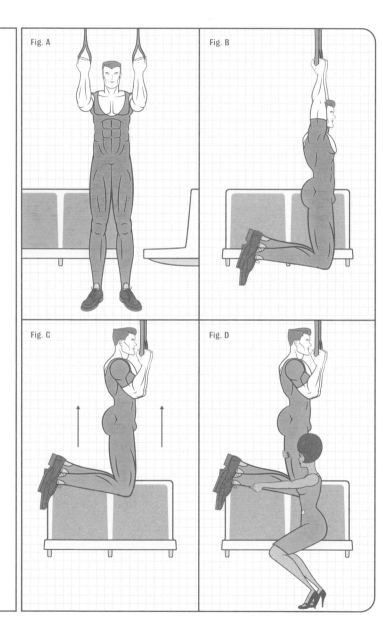

Fig. A

Fig. B

Fig. C

Fig. D

# TRAIN SEAT SUPER CRUNCHES

*Skill Level: Difficult*

1. Ask a friend to sit in the seat behind you.

2. Swing your legs up over the back of your chair, so that your knees fold over the top. (Fig. A)

3. Ask your friend to grip your ankles and hold your feet steady. (Fig. B)

4. Cross your arms over your chest and perform a set of 10 to 30 sit-ups (depending on your ability). (Fig. C)

5. When finished, switch positions with your friend, so she can do a set, too. (Fig. D) If the seat is too big or you are not tall enough, use a briefcase to boost your height as Judy has.

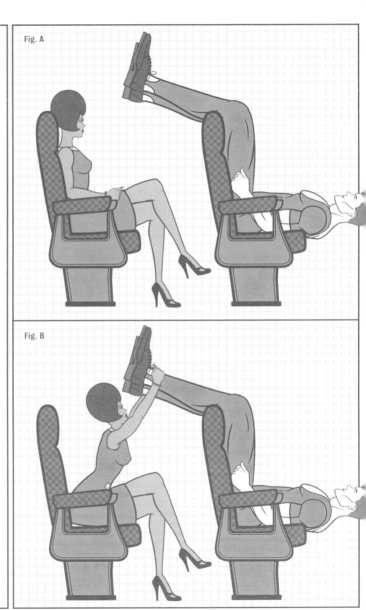

Fig. A

Fig. B

Fig. C

Fig. D

**8 min.** or longer

DURATION

# COMMUTER SEAT CHECK CHALLENGE #1

The good news: Your conductor will give you everything you need to solve this brainteaser as soon as you've paid your fare. The bad news: The proper solution to this puzzle will more or less obliterate any proof that you've actually paid your fare. The best solution: Tell the conductor of your plan before you begin.

## WHAT YOU'LL NEED:

Train seat check

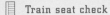

1. To solve this puzzle, you'll need a seat check that's at least one inch wide and two inches tall. If your seat check isn't big enough, attempt the brainteaser with a business card.

2. The goal is to bend and/or tear the seat check into a bracelet that can fit around your fist.

3. The bracelet must be a single, unbroken loop of paper. You may not use glue, scotch tape, or other adhesives.

4. Once you discover the solution to this trick, you can repeat the steps with an 8 1/2 x 11 sheet of paper—and end up with a loop wide enough to wrap around your waist!

*HINT #1: You only need to make 4 tears.*
*HINT #2: You only need to fold the stub once.*

*(See "Solutions," p. 84.)*

# COMMUTER SEAT CHECK CHALLENGE #2

8 min.
or longer

DURATION

You'll need six seat checks to solve this next puzzle—and part of the fun comes from hunting down six seat checks in your passenger car. Why not call upon five of your fellow passengers to join in the fun?

 **WHAT YOU'LL NEED:**

 Six seat checks

1. Arrange the seat checks on your snack tray as shown in Figure A. The first three should be face up, the last three should be bottom up, and there should be one empty slot in the middle.

2. Your goal is to switch the position of the seat checks so that the "tops" are on the right and the "bottoms" are on the left. (Fig. B)

3. Any check can move into an adjacent empty space or jump over adjacent checks into an empty space. (Fig. C)

4. You have but one restriction: "Tops" can only move to the right, and "bottoms" can only move to the left. (Fig. D)

*HINT: It will take at least 15 moves to solve the puzzle.*

*(See "Solutions," p. 84.)*

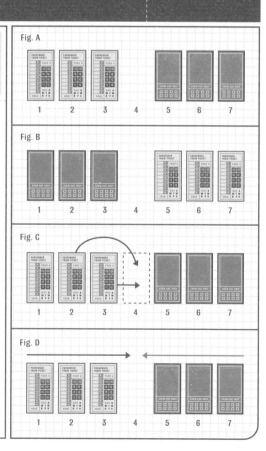

Fig. A

1  2  3  4  5  6  7

Fig. B

1  2  3  4  5  6  7

Fig. C

1  2  3  4  5  6  7

Fig. D

1  2  3  4  5  6  7

# COMMUTER SEAT CHECK CHALLENGE #3

**8 min.**
or longer

D U R A T I O N

You'll need a whopping 12 seat checks to solve this puzzle—and if there aren't that many passengers in your train car, consider yourself blessed. Just ask someone for a book of matches and use the matchsticks instead; they work just as well.

## WHAT YOU'LL NEED:

Twelve seat checks

-or-

Twelve matches

1. Arrange the seat checks or matches in the four-square diagram as shown in Figure A.

2. By moving simply three seat checks, can you end up with three squares?

*HINT: You'll need to destroy three squares to arrive at three squares.*

*(See "Solutions," p. 84.)*

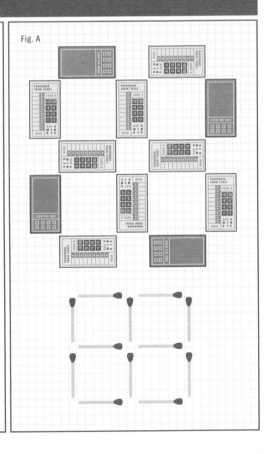

Fig. A

# PLAY CHEESE VERSUS CRACKERS

**3–7** min.

DURATION

Most train café cars offer a spectacular array of inedible, overpriced foods: rubbery chicken patties, super-salted peanuts, foul-smelling hot dogs, and worse. The smart commuter knows that these foods are not fit for human consumption. However, an inexpensive packet of cheese sandwich crackers will give you all the playing pieces for a wonderfully entertaining board game.

 WHAT YOU'LL NEED:

One packet of cheese sandwich crackers

Plastic knife

1. Take a seat in the café car with your opponent.

2. Unwrap the cheese sandwich crackers.

3. Use a plastic knife to separate the cheese from the crackers. You will need four cheese pieces and four crackers. (Fig. A)

4. Cheese goes first. This player should move a game piece to any of the eight free squares on the board. (See board on p. 87.)

5. Crackers goes next, placing a game piece in any of the remaining free squares.

6. This process repeats until all eight pieces are on the board.

7. Cheese should move any of its pieces to the available free space.

8. Then Crackers does the same.

9. Players continue alternating turns until someone gets three pieces in a row.

10. This person can eat the cheese and crackers—and the loser pays for the next game!

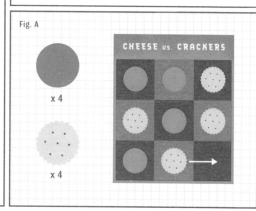

Fig. A

x 4

x 4

CHEESE vs. CRACKERS

# Ⅱ ELEVATOR WAITING GAMES

| | |
|---|---|
| 1 | Using the control panel, memorize the Braille patterns for the numbers 1 through 10. |
| 2 | Estimate the weight of all the passengers in your car. |
| 3 | Take the time to observe whether or not your elevator has a button for the 13th floor. |
| 4 | If not, ask any 14th-floor passengers about this curious omission. |
| 5 | Start timing your elevator rides with a stopwatch. Does the elevator travel faster with two passengers instead of 12? |
| 6 | Name the '74 skyscraper adventure whose name is an anagram of FINER GROWTH TEEN ION. (See "Solutions," p. 84.) |
| 7 | Sing along with the elevator music. |
| 8 | Encourage other passengers to join you. Conduct them with your umbrella. |
| 9 | As passengers step on board the elevator, ask if you can press the button for them. If they agree, pretend that the button is electrocuting you. |
| 10 | Determine how many of the elevator floors are prime numbers. |

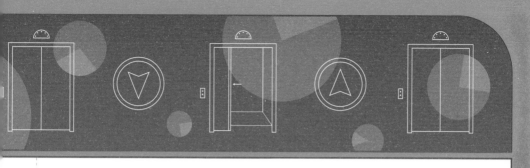

| 11 | Face the corner, and don't say anything to anyone. |
|----|----|
| 12 | Ask a fellow passenger if you can sit on his shoulders. Explain that you're with building maintenance and need to check the ventilation shaft. |
| 13 | Make a list of ten people you would love to be trapped in an elevator with. |
| 14 | Make a list of ten people you would hate to be trapped in an elevator with. |
| 15 | Say the following phrase ten times fast: "Lefty's lift lets lisping loons lull." |
| 16 | Pretend your elevator is like the great glass elevator near the end of *Charlie and the Chocolate Factory* and you can fly anywhere in the world. Where would you go? |
| 17 | When the elevator doors close, lean over to the person next to you and say, "Don't worry. They open again." |
| 18 | Estimate how much time you've spent in an elevator this year. |
| 19 | Estimate how much longer it would take to use the stairs instead. |
| 20 | Estimate how much weight you would lose by taking the stairs. |

# III

# AUTO AND BUS
## WAITING GAMES

Today's automobiles have more entertainment features than ever before—it's not uncommon to drive past SUVs with entertainment systems that rival my local cinema. But before you go out and plunk down five thousand dollars for a DVD player that runs off your cigarette lighter, consider the following activities—each of which can be performed for just a few dollars or less.

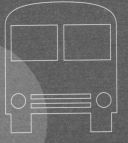

# GRAMMY BOWMAN'S TRAFFIC SIGN BINGO

**8 min.**
or longer

DURATION

My Grammy pioneered this game on bus trips to Atlantic City with her fellow senior citizens—and it's perfectly good fun for a bus or carpool full of commuters. For optimal results, use four players—and make sure all of them are smoking.

## WHAT YOU'LL NEED:

 Ten packs of Marlboros

 About 50 coins or bingo chips

✂ Scissors

1. Distribute the coins or bingo markers evenly among all players.

2. Cut out the bingo cards on pages 89–95, and distribute one to each player (except the driver, who will serve as judge).

3. Each player should put a dollar into the pot and place one coin or bingo marker on the "free space."

4. Players must watch the road signs. Each time they pass a sign with one of the words or numbers on their bingo cards, this square should be covered with a penny or bingo chip.

5. The first player to get five chips in a row (horizontally, vertically, or diagonally) is the winner. (Fig. A) He or she should yell out "Bingo!" The driver should verify the contestant's accuracy at the next red light.

6. Half of the pot should go to the winner. The other half should be donated to the religious organization of the winner's choice.

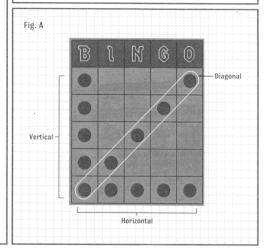

Fig. A

# RELAX WITH COMMUTER HEADREST SHIATSU

**8 min.**
or longer

DURATION

Do headaches and sinus problems leave your co-workers feeling down? Forget over-the-counter medications, and give Shiatsu a try. This Japanese form of stress relief uses pressure on common acupuncture points; some of its techniques are more than 4,000 years old. I can't really imagine what the ancient Japanese got so stressed about—it's not like they had traffic accidents and highway congestion to worry about—but if Shiatsu worked for them, it can work for you, too.

 WHAT YOU'LL NEED:

 A pair of hands

 An aching head

Fig. A

1. Your co-worker should sit directly in front of you in the front passenger seat. DO NOT use Shiatsu on the person driving your carpool; its effects are extremely relaxing and could lead to a traffic accident.

2. Your co-worker should recline her chair as much as possible, so that her head is almost resting in your lap. (Fig. A)

3. Comb your fingers through your co-worker's hair. Work back from the hairline so that your fingers brush over the entire scalp. (Fig. B)

Fig. B

*(Continued on the following pages)*

(4) Using your thumbs and forefingers, pinch lightly around the edges of the ears. This technique benefits the whole person, as the ears contain acupressure points for the entire body. Cover each ear twice. (Fig. C)

(5) Take one section of your partner's hair and tug gently. Repeat until you have covered all areas of her head. (Fig. D)

(6) Rest your fingers on your co-worker's temples, and rest your thumbs in the middle of the hairline. Then "walk" your thumbs toward the back, pressing firmly at one-inch intervals. (Fig. E)

(7) Gently pinch along your co-worker's eyebrows. (Fig. F)

(8) Press the small space between each eye and the bridge of the nose. Hold for several seconds. (Fig. G)

(9) Feel for a bony ridge near the outer end of each eyebrow. Press the points just outside this ridge and hold for several seconds. (Fig. H)

(10) Walk your fingers from the eyebrows out to the temples. Instead of pressing hard, gently rotate your fingertips. (Fig. I)

Now that your co-worker is completely relaxed, it would be rude to ask her to return the favor. But make sure she promises you a Shiatsu treatment for the ride back!

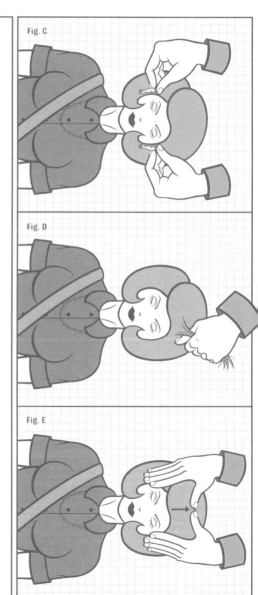

Fig. C

Fig. D

Fig. E

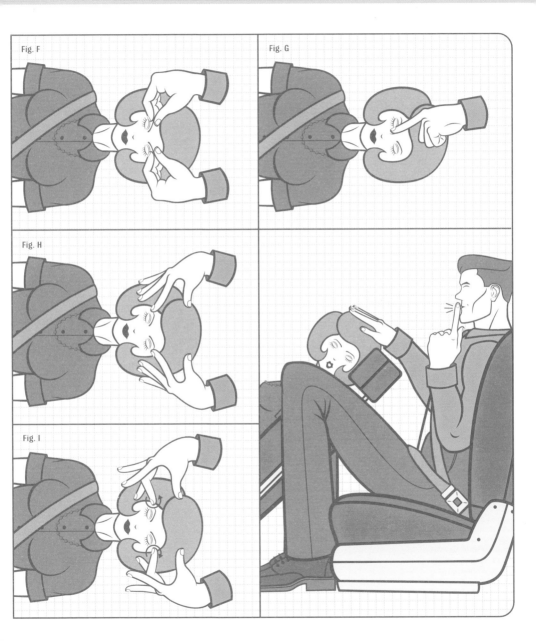

# HONK A MORSE CODE MESSAGE

**3 min.**
or less

DURATION

Many people believe that the cars of the future will include video screens that allow us to communicate with other drivers. But why bother? I've always believed that Morse code is an excellent way to convey messages. Although night drivers will prefer to use flashing high beams, I believe the message is stated more clearly by honking.

 **WHAT YOU'LL NEED:**

⊘ Car horn

◖⊱ High beams (optional)

① Using the chart below, honk or flash out a message of your own creation.

② Or use the pre-coded messages at right to brighten a fellow driver's day!

| . = short honk | ⁻ = long honk | M | -- | T | - |
|---|---|---|---|---|---|
| A | .- | G | --. | N | -. | U | ..- |
| B | -... | H | .... | O | --- | V | ...- |
| C | -.-. | I | .. | P | .--. | W | .-- |
| D | -.. | J | .--- | Q | --.- | X | -..- |
| E | . | K | -.- | R | .-. | Y | -.-- |
| F | ..-. | L | .-.. | S | ... | Z | --.. |

Have a Great Day!

I Like Your Smile!

Wow, Nice Car!

Your Bumper Stickers

Are Hilarious!

Pardon Me, but Your

(Left/Right) (Front/Rear)

Tire Looks a Little Low!

Be Careful! There Is an

Escaped Lunatic

with an Axe in

the Backseat of

Your Car!

# COMPOSE A TRAFFIC SIGN HAIKU

**3 min.**
or less

DURATION

As president of the Paramus, New Jersey, Society of Poets, I get most of my ideas while driving to and from the office; the tricky part is jotting them down without causing a multi-car accident. This dilemma inspired me to create Traffic Sign Haiku, ultra-short poems that you can compose in your mind while driving (and jot down when you reach a traffic light). All you need to begin is a clear mind and an inspirational road sign.

## WHAT YOU'LL NEED:

 Pencil

 Paper

1. As soon as you pass a traffic sign, begin composing. All words on the traffic sign must appear within your composition.

2. Remember that a haiku consists of 3 lines: a 5-syllable line, a 7-syllable line, and a 5-syllable line.

3. If you get stuck, feel free to build your own haiku from any of the phrases on the following page.

Here are four examples of my own traffic sign haiku:

**LIFE MOVES TOO FAST**
Reduce Speed Ahead.
Take time to relax. Your work
will always be there.

**TAKING A STAND**
No, I won't budge or
yield to oncoming traffic.
I have rights, too, friend.

**I CAN ONLY TAKE SO MUCH**
This load I carry
is sometimes too much to bear.
Danger: Falling Rock.

**HE'S NOTHING TO BE AFRAID OF**
Caution: Moose Crossing!
"Greetings, antlered quadruped!"
The wise beast smiles back.

## 5 SYLLABLES:

- A bald eagle soars
- Warning—slow down now!
- The first thaw of spring
- Gas, food, and lodging
- Cherry blossoms fall
- Wrong way: Turn back now
- The wind in the trees
- Congestion ahead
- Anticipation
- Weigh station next left

## 7 SYLLABLES:

- Service area keep right
- My bowl is full of warm rice
- Yield to oncoming traffic
- Like the laugh of a newborn
- Last exit before pay toll
- The graceful arc of a dove
- Left lane ends 1000 feet
- Morning dew tickles my toes
- No stopping on wet pavement
- Crafty fox—he always wins

# VANITY LICENSE PLATE PUZZLER

**3–7 min.**

DURATION

Nothing makes a morning bus ride go faster than spotting an enigmatic vanity license plate; the best ones involve tricky wordplay that requires miles and miles of driving time to work out. If you pay attention, you'll find plenty of these plates on the road—but if you need a quick fix, try matching the ten plates below with the ten people most likely to drive them. For example, the plate GU10TAG ("Gu-ten-tag") would most likely be owned by the German Ambassador. (See "Solutions," p. 85.)

German Ambassador

Jim Morrison Groupie

French Chef

Prizefighter

Angry Feminist

Star Wars Geek

Big Band Leader

Supermodel

Dental Hygienist

Pirate

# SUPER VANITY LICENSE PLATE PUZZLER

**8 min.**
or longer

DURATION

Now that you've cracked the first vanity license plate puzzler, you're ready for the ultimate challenge. I've hidden 20 of my favorite vanity license plates inside this puzzle grid; your task is to find them. To assist you, I'm also providing lists of difficult clues and easy clues. Answers are printed horizontally, vertically, and sometimes backward. Give yourself one point for each hard clue used and an additional two points for each easy clue used. And if you score below 50, consider yourself ready to work at the DMV! (See "Solutions," p. 85.)

## DIFFICULT CLUES:

1. A Christmas Carol—there's no L

2. Steve Martin catchphrase in the '70s: "Well, _____ _____!"

3. Are they fruits? Or vegetables?

4. To the rescue—as spoken by Inspector Clouseau

5. Straight A student's license plate

6. Valley girl's plate

7. Meet me at 5—and don't forget the beer!

8. John McEnroe's car

9. Look on the bright side; popular song of the '40s

10. Friend of the Three Little Bears

11. Physician of Derek Jeter, Mario Lemieux, Dan Marino, and their friends

12. Seen on an ophthalmologist's car

13. Seen on an accountant's car

14. Seize the night

15. Seen on an Australian import

16. Seen on a radiologist's car

17. Common trait of artists

18. Common request among photographers

19. License plate of a massage therapist

20. Three Stooges fan

## EASY CLUES:

1. Noel
2. Excuse me
3. Tomatoes
4. "To zee rescue!"
5. Perfect GPA
6. Fer shure
7. 5PM: Bring your own beer
8. Tennis pro
9. Accentuate the positive
10. Goldilocks
11. Doctor for jocks
12. Dr. Eyeballs
13. Calculator
14. Carpe piem
15. G'day, mate!
16. See through you
17. Creative
18. S-mile
19. I knead you
20. Nyuk! Nyuk! Nyuk!

## PUZZLE GRID

| C | + | D | 8 | 2 | N | X | A | A | X |
|---|---|---|---|---|---|---|---|---|---|
| 9 | R | S | C | A | L | Q | L | 8 | R |
| Q | 2 | M | 8 | O | S | Q | 3 | 2 | A |
| U | Z | I | E | R | U | S | 4 | 5 | U |
| C | R | E | 8 | I | V | M | – | P | Y |
| T | E | C | A | R | P | E | P | M | L |
| H | S | 9 | D | X | 3 | + | I | B | O |
| R | Q | T | R | O | X | 8 | K | Y | K |
| U | 1 | H | I | J | K | M | N | O | S |
| U | O | O | B | 4 | U | Y | E | B | 5 |
| 5 | S | O | A | C | Y | A | A | W | Z |
| 9 | P | 3 | L | O | N | D | D | 7 | 8 |
| R | R | + | Z | D | + | G | U | G | O |
| S | O | X | 9 | 9 | X | 2 | 2 | S | F |
| 3 | A | P | G | O | O | 4 | D | T | T |

**3 min.**
or less

D U R A T I O N

# COMMUTER I.D. DRIVING GAME

As a commuter, I see many of the same drivers day after day—and even though I've never exchanged words with them, I've imagined their personal lives in great detail. On one occasion, I've even followed a person to her job to determine if I was right. This almost resulted in unpleasant legal consequences, so you have to be careful. If you want to speculate about people, try this game instead.

## WHAT YOU'LL NEED:

Pencil

Paper

(1) Approach your target car from behind.

(2) Have one of your passengers record the car's license plate.

(3) Now pull alongside the driver so that all passengers can take a good look at him or her.

(4) The goal is to use every letter in the license plate to describe the driver. For example, let's say you pass a hearse with the license plate YUG4 3TC, and the driver looks 19 years old and ready to fall asleep. Possible answers could be "Young Undertaker Going to Cemetery" or even "Yawning Ugly Guy Turns Curve."

(5) As the driver, you get to decide the best answer; special consideration should be given to any answers that incorporate letters *and* numbers.

MSW-2BR = Man Shaving With Two-Bladed Razor

# CONDUCT A COMMUTER BUS ORCHESTRA

**8 min.**
or longer

Radio can provide an excellent diversion on your way to work—provided, of course, that you can tolerate all of the annoying morning drive-time disc jockeys. But if you're tired of listening to a Walkman on your bus every morning, pull off those headphones and lead your fellow commuters in beautiful compositions of your own creation. Here's everything you need to make your own four-piece bus orchestra.

 WHAT YOU'LL NEED:

Two plastic drinking straws

One iced Frappuccino

Two credit cards

One business card

Tape

Scissors

## DRINKING STRAW OBOE

(1) Cut one end of the straw as shown in Fig. A. The ends of the straw will function as double reeds.

(2) If you blow through the straw and don't hear a sound, the ends are probably too far apart; pinch them together with your lips and blow. (Fig. B)

(3) Use the scissors to cut small holes in the top of the straw. The holes should be about one inch apart. (Fig. C)

(4) Placing your fingers over the holes will alter the sound of the oboe. (Fig. D)

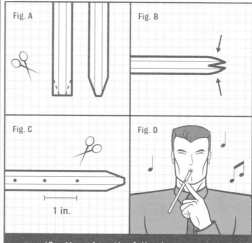

Fig. A

Fig. B

Fig. C

1 in.

Fig. D

*(Continued on the following pages)*

## ICED FRAPPUCCINO WOODWIND

I've only attempted this with an iced Frappuccino ordered to go from Starbucks, but it probably works with any drink served in a plastic cup with a snap-on lid.

1. Drink the beverage until there are only one or two inches left at the bottom. (Fig. E)

2. Hold the straw between your thumb and index finger, and blow across the top of the straw. With a little practice, you should hear a high-pitched, clear sound. (Fig. F)

3. Moving the straw up and down in the liquid will change the pitch. The higher the straw, the lower the pitch—and vice versa. (Fig. G)

## CREDIT CARD BUGLE

1. Take two plastic credit cards and tape the sides as shown. Make sure the credit cards do not lie flat against each other; there should be about an eighth of an inch of wiggle room. (Fig. H)

2. Slip a business card between the two credit cards. (Fig. I)

3. Press your lips against the credit cards and blow. Like the end of the Drinking Straw Oboe, the two credit cards will function as a double reed—but the sound is fuller, deeper, and more resonant, like a bugle. Adjusting the business card will raise or lower the tone. (Fig. J)

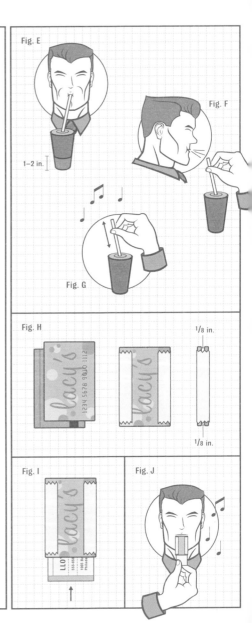

Fig. E

Fig. F

1–2 in.

Fig. G

Fig. H

1/8 in.

1/8 in.

Fig. I

Fig. J

## WINDOW PERCUSSION

A quick look inside your briefcase or purse should yield dozens of tools for enhancing your percussion section. Encourage your drummer to try different lipsticks, combs, hairbrushes, Binaca canisters, the works.

## ORCHESTRATION

Once you have an oboe, bugle, woodwind, and percussion section, you're ready to play—

but until everyone masters their instruments, you may want to ask the bus driver to turn on the radio, so you can jam along with today's hottest hits. The following songs are particularly well suited for commuting orchestras:

*Sometimes When We Touch* – Dan Hill
*Glory of Love* – Peter Cetera
*Tonight I Celebrate My Love* – Peabo Bryson
*Ain't It Funny* – J. Lo and Ja Rule
*I Honestly Love You* – Olivia Newton-John
*Muskrat Love* – Captain & Tennille

**8 min.**
or more

D U R A T I O N

# PLAY COMMUTER WAITING GAMES I-SPY

This variation of "I-Spy" has been tailored for the typical commuter bus or carpool; each player should study the list before beginning the trip, then compete to amass the most points before reaching your office. Solo commuters can compete against themselves in an attempt to beat their "personal best."

## WHAT YOU'LL NEED:

Pencil

Paper

(1) Each player should study the list before the drive.

(2) Here are the items your eyes need to spy:

| ITEMS: | POINTS: |
|---|---|
| Driver picking his/her nose | 5 |
| Woman putting on makeup while driving | 3 |
| Man putting on makeup while driving | 7 |

| ITEMS: | POINTS: |
|---|---|
| Person talking on cell phone while driving | 3 |
| Person shouting on cell phone while driving | 4 |
| Person attempting to spread butter or cream cheese on bagel while driving | 5 |

| ITEMS: | POINTS: | ITEMS: | POINTS: |
|---|---|---|---|
| Vanity license plate | 4 | Car with dog or cat in backseat | 3 |
| Indecipherable vanity license plate | 5 | Car with any other animal in backseat | 4 |
| Fuzzy dice | 5 | Roadkill | 5 |
| 18-wheeler with silhouette of sexy woman on mudflaps | 5 | Person using shoulder lane as personal restroom | 5 |
| 18-wheeler with Yosemite Sam on mudflaps | 5 | Toll plaza | 1 |
| Bumper sticker claiming that the driver's child is an honor student | 4 | Person stepping out of car at toll plaza to retrieve change that was incorrectly thrown into the toll basket | 5 |
| Bumper sticker supporting or condemning *Roe vs. Wade* | 7 | Driver in EZ Pass Lane causing widespread chaos after realizing at last possible moment that he/she does not have EZ Pass | 5 |

# BIKING AND WALKING WAITING GAMES

**IV**

**1** Count the number of steps in your commute.

**2** Redesign the traffic light.

**3** Avoid every crack in the sidewalks.

**4** Invent a headline for today's newpaper. Check the nearest vending box to see if you're correct.

**5** Which '75 Aerosmith song is an anagram of the words THAW WAIL SKY. (See "Solutions," p. 85.)

**6** Calculate the amount of calories you'll burn while biking to work (consider that 30 minutes of moderately paced biking will burn about 346 calories).

**7** Calculate the amount of calories you'll burn walking to work (consider that 30 minutes of briskly paced walking will burn about 200 calories).

**8** Calculate the amount of calories you'll burn sitting at a desk all day (consider that 30 minutes of sitting will burn about 42 calories).

**9** Try to guess exactly how much money you're carrying—down to the last cent. Open your wallet to determine if you're correct.

**10** Put business cards in your spokes for a convincing "revving" sound.

| 11 | Name the "pedestrian" celebrity whose name is an anagram of the words CARTWHEEL HORN SKIP. (See "Solutions," p. 85.) |
| 12 | Strike up a conversation with a nearby pedestrian. |
| 13 | Determine which celebrity would have a cameo role as this nearby pedestrian in a Hollywood epic based on your life. |
| 14 | Determine what the title might be for a Hollywood epic based on your life. |
| 15 | Ask your fellow pedestrian if he/she has seen the trailers for this epic. When he/she says no, proceed to describe your entire life to date. |
| 16 | Guess the age of each passing commuter. |
| 17 | Guess nicknames for each passing commuter. |
| 18 | Guess the sexual orientation of each passing commuter. |
| 19 | Estimate today's temperature in degrees Fahrenheit. |
| 20 | Convert your estimate of today's temperature to degrees Kelvin ([$5/9$ x temperature Fahrenheit] + 305.16). |

# AIRPLANE
## WAITING GAMES

With airlines cutting costs left and right, entertainment and amusing diversions are often the first expenses to be sacrificed. But the creative commuter doesn't depend on flimsy headphones or in-flight movies for fun. After all, why waste two hours watching the latest Meg Ryan schmaltz-fest when you could be building a spectacular airline blanket fort? Why listen to John Tesh when you could be doing *anything* other than listening to John Tesh? In airports and on airplanes, there's always something fun to do.

**8 min.**
or more

DURATION

# DO THE AIRPORT CHECK-IN LIMBO

Back when I was a student at Paramus Township High School, I won the limbo contest at our Spring Formal, which was a giant costume party for all of the seniors. My date, Jenny Solasky, and I were dressed as a pair of moose (par-a-mus, get it?), and if you think doing the limbo is tough, just try doing it with giant antlers strapped to your head. Needless to say, I'm pretty good, and I keep up my practice while waiting on line at the airport.

## WHAT YOU'LL NEED:

Airline check-in ropes

The best time to practice is while waiting in line at the baggage checks.

 Adjust the crowd-control ropes so that they are as high as possible. Place the poles far enough away from each other so that the ropes are taut. (Fig. A)

 Invite your fellow passengers to participate. Sponsor a prize as an incentive—try offering something from your luggage, such as a company pen or some moisturizing cream. (Fig. B)

**3** Each player should "limbo" under the rope in order of their position in the line. If a player touches the rope with any part of his body, he is disqualified. (Fig. C)

 After all of the players have passed under once, the rope should be lowered three inches, and play continues.

TIPS:
Bend your knees and lean forward. Most people lose the limbo contest because they fall backward. By leaning forward, you can control your center of gravity.

Notice the way Lloyd keeps his feet at least 18 inches apart, with toes pointing outward in opposite directions. (Fig. D) This concentrates his center of gravity and reduces his chances of toppling over.

Keep your arms close to your body—again, to concentrate your center of gravity.

Aim high—or low, that is. According to *The Guinness Book of World Records*, a West Indies woman named Teresa Marquis did the limbo in 1970 under a bar that was *six and a half inches high*!

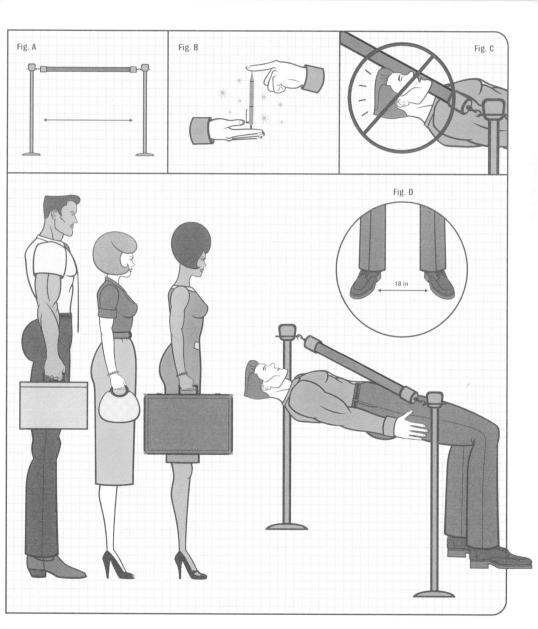

Fig. A

Fig. B

Fig. C

Fig. D

18 in

# MAKE AN AIRPLANE BLANKET FORT

**DURATION**

3-7 min.

For years, airlines have made a practice of overbooking flights by at least 15 percent to ensure there's never a single empty seat on any flight. This kind of sardine packing will cause many passengers to experience claustrophobia—but you can minimize this anxiety by creating your own coach class hideaway. It's the perfect place to conduct secret business transactions or just get a little quiet time. (This particular design works best in an aisle seat.)

## WHAT YOU'LL NEED:

 3 airline blankets

(1) Open the overhead compartment directly above your seat. (Fig. A)

(2) Wedge the top corners of two blankets under some heavy luggage. (Fig. B)

(3) Close the compartment door. (Fig. C)

(4) Let the two blankets fall on either side of your chair. (Fig. D)

(5) Stuff the end of the inner blanket between your seat cushion and the one next to you. (Fig. E)

(6) Stuff one end of the third blanket under the seat tray behind your chair. (Don't be afraid to ask the passenger behind you for her help.) (Fig. F)

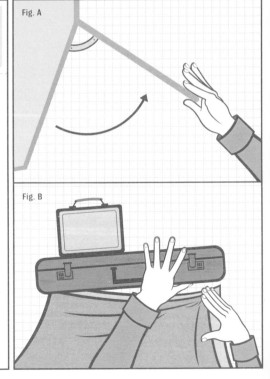

Fig. A

Fig. B

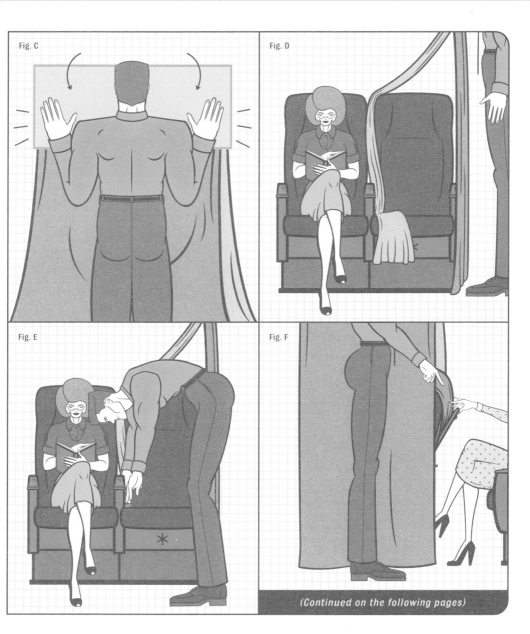

Fig. C

Fig. D

Fig. E

Fig. F

*(Continued on the following pages)*

(7) Ask the person in front of you to lean forward, and tuck the other end of the blanket behind her head. Request that she not get up for the remainder of the flight. (Fig. G)

(8) The blanket closest to the aisle functions as your door. Pull it back to enter the fort. (Fig. H)

Now enjoy the rest of the flight without any further interruptions! (Fig. I)

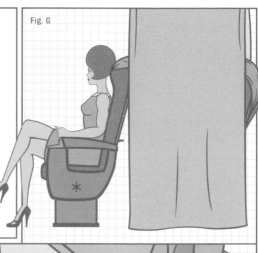

Fig. G

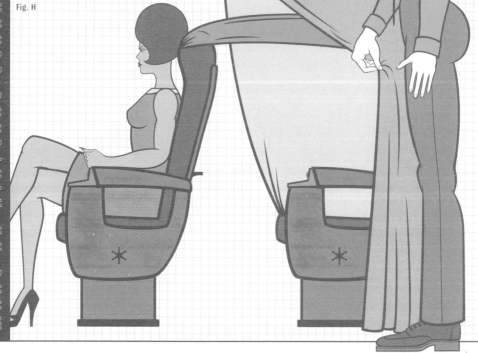

Fig. H

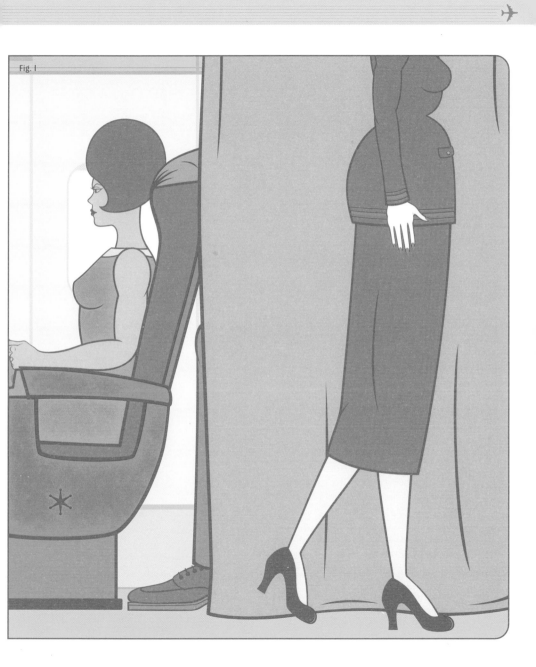

Fig. I

# RELAX WITH COMMUTER AIRLINE YOGA

**3–7 min.** each

DURATION

With their recycled air, miserable food, and cramped quarters, commuter airlines are a tremendous drain on the human body. If you want to survive (and thrive) as a frequent flyer, remember to exercise on the day of your flight, drink lots of water, avoid caffeinated and alcoholic beverages, eat easy-to-digest foods, and take occasional walks around the cabin. I also recommend the following yoga exercises, which can be performed in your seat or at various locations around the plane.

 WHAT YOU'LL NEED:

 Leotard

## WAITING FOR THE BATHROOM STRETCH

1. Stand facing the door to the restroom or a cabin wall. (Fig. A)

2. Place your palms and forearms flush against the wall, with fingers spread and pointing upward. Your feet should be planted about 12 inches apart. Notice how Lloyd's upper arms remain parallel to the floor. (Fig. B)

3. Keeping your hands and arms steady, twist at the waist, turning your torso to the right. (Fig. C)

4. Raise your left knee across your body so that your thigh is (more or less) parallel to the floor. Make sure your thigh and the joints under your index and third fingers are flush against the wall. (Fig. D)

5. Turn your head to the left, as far as you can. (Fig. E)

6. Hold this pose for at least 20 seconds, breathing gently.

7. Don't let rude remarks from surly flight attendants diminish your tranquility. (Fig. F)

8. Repeat on the other side.

(Continued on the following pages)

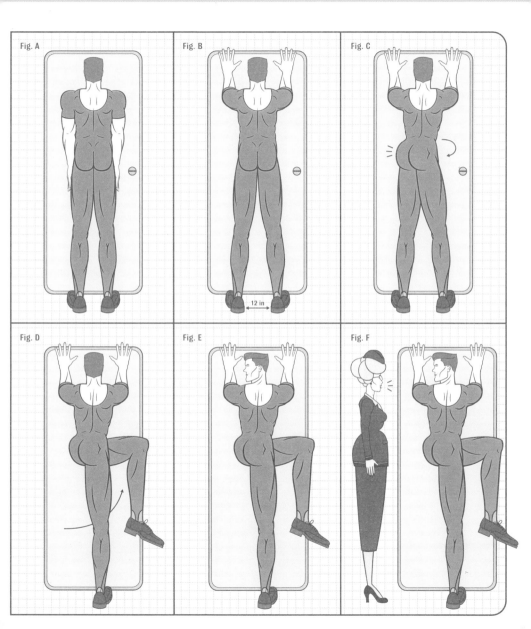

Fig. A

Fig. B

12 in

Fig. C

Fig. D

Fig. E

Fig. F

## FORGOT TO BRING A SWEATER STRETCH

1. While seated, loosen your seat-belt and remove your shoes. (Figs. A–B)

2. Inhaling, lift your right foot with both hands and raise your knee toward your chest. Keep your foot limp and lift your breastbone. Your back should be straight. (Fig. C)

3. Squeeze the knee to your chest while exhaling. (Fig. D)

4. Release the knee as you inhale, then repeat. (Fig. E)

5. After three lifts, switch to your left foot.

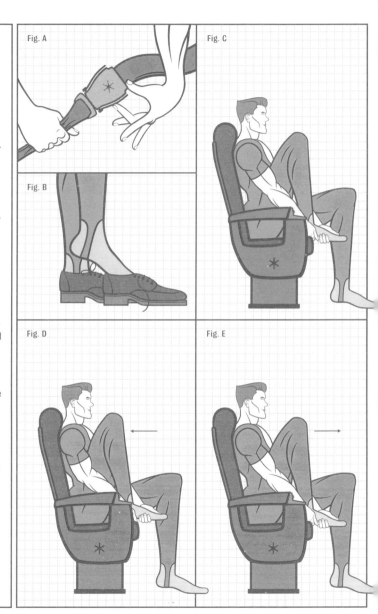

Fig. A

Fig. B

Fig. C

Fig. D

Fig. E

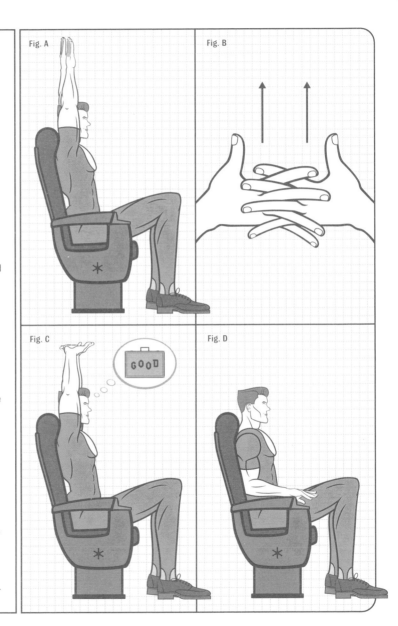

## REACH FOR THE OVERHEAD COMPARTMENT STRETCH

1. While seated, inhale and raise your arms straight overhead, so your elbows are in line with your ears. (Fig. A)

2. While exhaling, interlace your fingers and turn your wrists. Your palms now should be facing the overhead compartments. Keep them in this position. (Fig. B)

3. Inhale again while stretching your arms upward as high as you can reach. Imagine you are reaching for a bag stored in the overhead compartment. Visualize the bag as containing all the goodness of the universe. (Fig. C)

4. Relax, drop your arms, and exhale. (Fig. D)

5. Repeat steps 1 through 4 three times.

Fig. A

Fig. B

Fig. C

GOOD

Fig. D

# PLAY A GAME OF SAFETY CARD VOLLEYRACKET

**8 min.** or longer

I first participated in this game six years ago, while circling for three hours in a thick fog over Newark International Airport. The pilot said there was some kind of problem with the landing gear doohickey, but we were all having too much fun to pay much attention. Safety Card Volleyracket works for six or sixty players—and if your flight attendants seem game, invite them to serve as referees!

 **WHAT YOU'LL NEED:**

One airline safety card per player

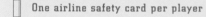 *SkyMall* magazine

(1) Open *SkyMall* magazine and find the page with the most useless product. (This can be a rather long activity in itself—if you can't decide, look for the page with the $150 Deluxe Canvas Grocery Bag.) (Fig. A)

(2) Tear out this page and crumple it into a ball. (Fig. B)

(3) Passengers should divide into two teams, on either side of the aisle. Ideally, you'll want teams of nine players each, but the game can be played with teams as small as two players each. (Fig. C)

(4) Each player should have an airline safety card. It should be folded closed and gripped in one hand like a badminton racket. (Fig. D)

(5) The team providing the ball is awarded the first serve, and the person in Position 1 begins the game. He serves by throwing the ball straight up and then swatting it over the net (the aisle) with his safety card. Other players may assist in swatting it over. If the opposing team fails to return the ball, the serving team scores one point (and keeps control of the serve). (Figs. E–F)

(6) If the serving team fails to return the ball, the opposing team scores one point (and gains control of the serve).

(7) Whenever a team regains possession of the serve, players must rotate positions in the direction shown on the chart. (Fig. G) If the "Fasten Seatbelts" sign is lit, players should remain in position (but continue playing) until the sign goes out.

(8) The game lasts to 21 points, and the winning team must win by two.

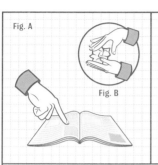

Fig. A

Fig. B

Fig. C

Team 1

| 1 | 2 | 3 | 4 | 5 | 6 | 7 | 8 | 9 |

AISLE

| 1 | 2 | 3 | 4 | 5 | 6 | 7 | 8 | 9 |

Team 2

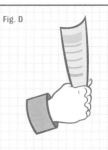

Fig. D

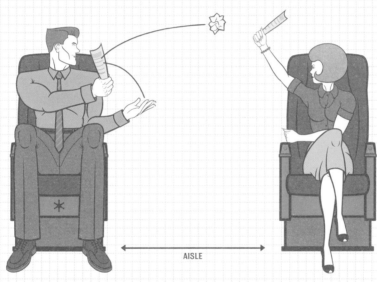

Fig. E

AISLE

Fig. F

Team 1

| 1 | 2 | 3 | 4 | 5 | 6 | 7 | 8 | 9 |

AISLE

| 1 | 2 | 3 | 4 | 5 | 6 | 7 | 8 | 9 |

Team 2

Fig. G

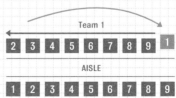

Team 1

| 2 | 3 | 4 | 5 | 6 | 7 | 8 | 9 | 1 |

AISLE

| 1 | 2 | 3 | 4 | 5 | 6 | 7 | 8 | 9 |

Team 2

# STAGE AN IN-FLIGHT MOVIE PUPPET SHOW

**8 min.** or longer

DURATION

Nothing makes a cross-country flight go faster than a good in-flight movie—but some airlines charge five, seven, even up to ten dollars for headphone rentals! If you're traveling on business, you can bill these expenses to your company—but what about the cramped coach class passengers seated behind you? These people deserve some quality entertainment, too.

 **WHAT YOU'LL NEED:**

 In-flight magazine

 Plastic forks

 Socks

 Airsickness bag

 Toothpicks

 Olives

 Markers or pens

(1) Open your airline magazine to the description of the in-flight movie. Chances are, you'll find photographs of the actors and actresses starring in the film. (Fig. A)

(2) Tear out the faces of these stars. (Fig. B)

(3) Place the faces between the prongs of your forks. (Fig. C)

(4) If you can't find a photograph of a key actor, draw the person's face on an airsickness bag as shown. (Fig. D)

(5) For dragons, sharks, and other creatures involving special effects, be creative. Get two olives and a pair of toothpicks from the beverage cart.

(6) Spear the olives through the toothpicks. (Fig. E)

(7) Pull a sock over your hand, and spear the toothpicks in the front as "eyes." (Fig. F)

(8) You're ready to put on a show no one will ever forget. For character-driven films like *My Dinner with Andre*, you should have no trouble performing all of the roles by yourself. But for blockbuster epics like *Star Wars: Attack of the Clones*, enlist the help of your fellow passengers. (Fig. G) Ask the pilot to announce a casting call at the rear of the plane, and you'll have dozens of bored volunteers ready to audition.

Fig. A

Fig. B

Fig. C

Fig. D

Fig. E

Fig. F

Fig. G

# TEAR A DECK OF AIRLINE PLAYING CARDS IN HALF

**3 min.**
or less

DURATION

In recent years, airlines have become increasingly more restrictive, with bans on cigarette smoking and dozens of new security precautions. Yet at press time no major airline has taken any steps to prevent small children from harassing the passengers seated in front of them. Now I don't know about you, but I'd much rather inhale second-hand smoke than sit in front of a hyperactive four-year-old who keeps opening and closing his seat tray. Next time you find yourself near a hyper-kinetic tyke, try this simple demonstration to make Junior back off:

 **WHAT YOU'LL NEED:**

♠ One deck of airline playing cards

☺ One small hyper child

1. Ask the flight attendant for a deck of playing cards. Most commercial airlines provide these for free. (Fig. A)

2. Remove the cards from the pack, show them to the annoying child, and ask if he would like to play a game. (Fig. B)

3. Notice how Lloyd has the cards squared perfectly. Grip the cards in your left hand with your thumb and fingers at the bottom. (Fig. C)

4. Lift your right hand toward the top of the deck and rest the ball of your right thumb against the front of the deck. Your remaining fingers will rest against the back of the deck. (Fig. D)

5. While keeping the grip of your left hand steady, pull the top of the cards toward you with your right hand. (Fig. E)

6. If the cards do not slip, the first pull should break the deck halfway. A second pull should break the deck in half. (Fig. F)

7. Scatter the torn cards around the stunned child and return to your seat. This activity may invoke rude stares from surrounding grown-up passengers, but I guarantee that Junior will stop kicking the back of your seat. (Fig. G)

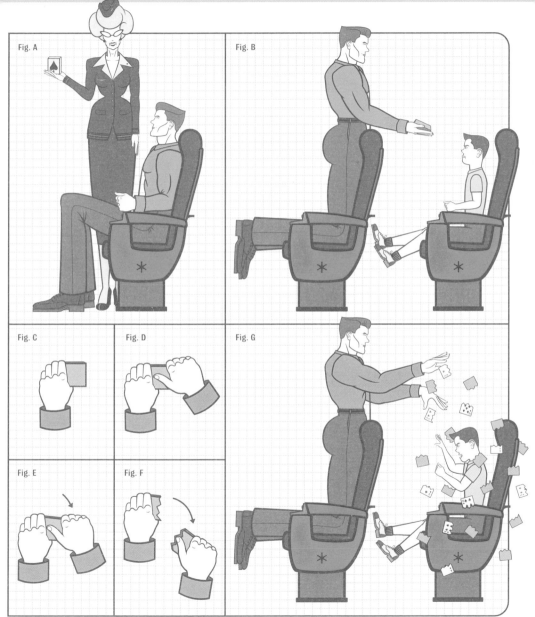

Fig. A

Fig. B

Fig. C

Fig. D

Fig. E

Fig. F

Fig. G

# DELIGHT CHILD PASSENGERS WITH SHADOW PUPPETS

**DURATION** 3–7 min.

Last month, I was on a plane with my eight-year-old nephew when the flight attendant announced that the in-flight movie was *Monsters, Inc.* Naturally, I was outraged; I knew that the sight of Halle Berry and Billy Bob Thornton making love would traumatize my nephew for life. So I immediately brought him to the back of the plane and entertained him with shadow puppets for the next two hours.

## WHAT YOU'LL NEED:

Access to overhead lights

Flashlight (optional)

(1) Stand up and announce that you have a special surprise for all of your fellow passengers. (Fig. A)

(2) Request that they turn off their overhead lights and close their window shades, to make the cabin as dark as possible. (Fig. B)

(3) Turn on an overhead light in your row that is farthest from your window. If possible, angle the bulb so it points toward the window screen. (Fig. C)

(4) If your overhead light is not adjustable, ask a flight attendant for a flashlight. All airplane cabins store flashlights in the event of an emergency. Explain that your wedding ring has dropped onto the floor and you wish to find it without disturbing your fellow passengers. Or, if you feel comfortable, invite the flight attendant to participate in your show by aiming the light against the plastic shade. (Fig. D)

(5) Create your puppet show with the diagrams shown in Figure E.

(6) Enhance your performance with funny animal sounds.

(7) Respond to applause with deep and sincere bows.

Fig. A

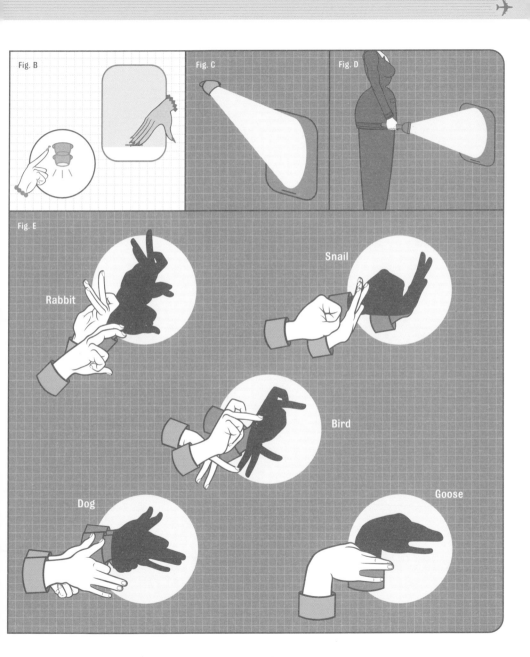

Fig. B

Fig. C

Fig. D

Fig. E

Rabbit

Snail

Bird

Dog

Goose

# PAPPY BOWMAN'S OLDE-TYME TRAY-SLAPPING CONTEST

**3 min.** or less

DURATION

The very first time I flew on an airplane, I was six years old—and my great-grandfather Herbert "Pappy" Bowman showed me how to play this game, which is an old favorite of World War II veterans and other members of the Greatest Generation. Some say its origins date back to nineteenth-century stagecoaches, a popular mode of transportation for early American commuters.

  **WHAT YOU'LL NEED:**

 Steady hands

☺ Gumption

Before takeoff, review these instructions with all of the contestants seated in your row (you'll need a minimum of two players, but up to eight people can enjoy this game).

1. The flight attendants will ask all passengers to secure their trays in the upright position. These trays should remain upright, even after the "Fasten Seatbelts" sign has been turned off.

2. Once the plane reaches cruising altitude, the flight attendants will enter the aisle with beverage carts. All players in your row must place their hands in their laps.

3. The signal to "draw" comes as soon as the flight attendant begins speaking to any of the contestants. Players must then strike out at the latch on their dinner tray.

4. The person with the first tray to open is the winner.

In the nineteenth century, losers would be tossed out of the stagecoach to fend for themselves in the savage terrain of the Wild West. Nowadays, they just fork over their desserts to the winner.

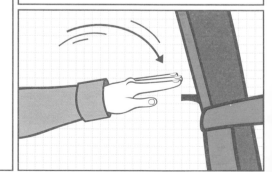

# CROWN YOUR FAVORITE FLIGHT ATTENDANT

There's a special place in my heart for flight attendants. They bring me drinks when I'm thirsty, they offer me food when I'm hungry, and they give me blankets when I want to build a blanket fort. This next activity lets us honor the brave men and women who fly the friendly skies.

 **WHAT YOU'LL NEED:**

 *SkyMall* magazine (or any airline magazine)

① Remove the staples from the spine of the magazine, so you can pull its pages apart without tearing them. (Fig. A)

② Take any two-page spread and gently lift it out of the magazine. (Fig. B)

③ Carefully tear this page in half, so you are left with a sheet of paper approximately 8 ½ x 11 inches. (Fig. C)

Fig. B

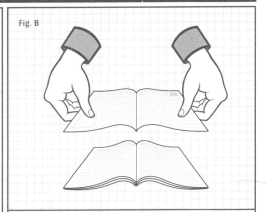

Fig. C

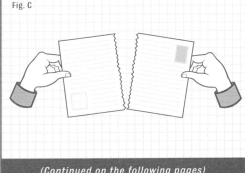

Fig. A

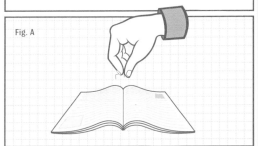

*(Continued on the following pages)*

CROWN YOUR FAVORITE FLIGHT ATTENDANT (continued)

(4) Fold the paper from top to bottom as shown in Figure D.

(5) Fold the paper from right to left just enough to make a crease near the top— as shown in Figure E.

(6) Fold the right corner down to meet the crease. (Fig. F)

(7) Repeat with the left corner. (Fig. G)

(8) Lift the two flaps up. (Figs. H–I)

(9) Separate the crown flaps, bestow the crown upon your favorite flight attendant, and thank her or him for making your flight such a special one. For the remainder of the trip, refer to this person only as "your majesty." (Fig. J)

Fig. F

Fig. G

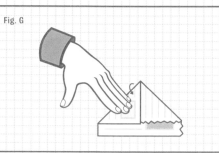

Fig. H

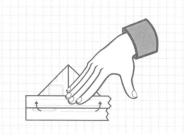

Fig. D

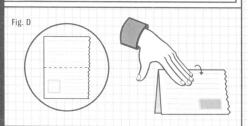

Fig. E

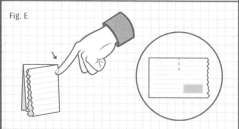

Fig. I

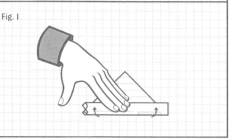

# SOLUTIONS

## PLAY "NAME THAT TRAIN" (pp. 18–21)

EASY PUZZLE #1 (MUSIC) · "The Chattanooga Choo Choo"
EASY PUZZLE #2 (LITERATURE) · *The Little Engine That Could*
MEDIUM PUZZLE #1 (LITERATURE) · *Murder on the Orient Express*
MEDIUM PUZZLE #2 (MOVIES) · *The Silver Streak*
DIFFICULT PUZZLE #1 (TELEVISION) · *Soul Train*
DIFFICULT PUZZLE #2 (TELEVISION) · *Supertrain*

## WHAT'S WRONG WITH THIS TRAIN STATION (p. 22)

Aside from the most *obvious* mistakes:

1. The commuters are boarding the train in an orderly and effective single-file line.

2. There is no large gap between the train and the platform where valuable items might fall.

3. The businessman is allowing the woman with the baby to step ahead of him.

4. The baby is not crying.

5. No one is speaking on a cell phone.

6. The book being read by the businessman does not contain the leadership secrets of the retired CEO of a Fortune 500 company.

7. The businesswoman, upon recognizing the "No Smoking" sign, has extinguished her cigarette.

8. The 6:15 train is on the platform at 6:15.

9. The conductor appears to be providing useful information about the location of the train.

10. The litter on the train platform is missing.

## ELEVATOR WAITING GAMES (p. 36)

FINER GROWTH TEEN ION = THE TOWERING INFERNO

## COMMUTER SEAT CHECK CHALLENGE #1 (p. 32)

1. Fold the stub in half (from top to bottom) as shown.

2. Starting at the left side of the fold, make a vertical tear until you almost reach the bottom.

3. Starting at the right side of the fold, make a vertical tear until you almost reach the bottom.

4. Starting at the bottom middle, tear up until you almost reach the top.

5. Tear the middle half of the top fold.

6. Pull out into a big loop.

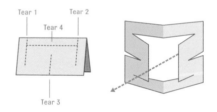

## COMMUTER SEAT CHECK CHALLENGE #2 (p. 33)

Move 3 to 4; move 5 to 3; move 6 to 5; move 4 to 6;
move 2 to 4; move 1 to 2; move 3 to 1; move 5 to 3;
move 7 to 5; move 6 to 7; move 4 to 6; move 2 to 4;
move 3 to 2; move 5 to 3; move 4 to 5.

## COMMUTER SEAT CHECK CHALLENGE #3 (p. 34)

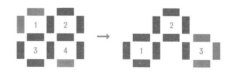

# SOLUTIONS

## VANITY LICENSE PLATE PUZZLER (p. 48)

GU10TAG (German Ambassador—Guten Tag)

II-M8TY (Pirate—Aye, aye, Matey!)

SIQTDE (Supermodel—QT in SIDE)

UUUD444 (Star Wars Geek—U's de Fours [Luke])

IRIGHTI (Prizefighter—RIGHT between the I's)

RATA2E (French Chef—Ratatouille)

OPN-WYD (Dental hygienist—Open wide)

A1-ANA2 (Big Band Leader—A one and a two)

H20MEN4 (Angry Feminist—Water men for?)

LVME-2X (Jim Morrison Groupie—Love me two times)

## SUPER VANITY LICENSE PLATE PUZZLER (p. 50)

| C | + | D | 8 | 2 | N | X | A | A | X |
|---|---|---|---|---|---|---|---|---|---|
| 9 | R | S | C | A | L | Q | L | 8 | R |
| Q | 2 | M | 8 | O | S | Q | 3 | 2 | A |
| U | Z | I | E | R | U | S | 4 | 5 | U |
| C | R | E | 8 | I | V | M | – | P | Y |
| T | E | C | A | R | P | E | P | M | L |
| H | S | 9 | D | X | 3 | + | I | B | O |
| R | Q | T | R | O | X | 8 | K | Y | K |
| U | 1 | H | I | J | K | M | N | O | S |
| U | O | O | B | 4 | U | Y | E | B | 5 |
| 5 | S | O | A | C | Y | A | A | W | Z |
| 9 | P | 3 | L | O | N | D | D | 7 | 8 |
| R | R | + | Z | D | + | G | U | G | O |
| S | O | X | 9 | 9 | X | 2 | 2 | S | F |
| 3 | A | P | G | O | O | 4 | D | T | T |

1.  HIJKMNO (Noel; there's no L)
2.  XQQSME (Excuse me)
3.  2M8OS (Tomatoes)
4.  2ZRESQ (To zee rescue!)
5.  400GPA (4.00 Grade Point Average)
6.  4SURE (Fer sure)
7.  5PMBYOB (Five o'clock, bring your own beer)
8.  10SPRO (Tennis pro)
9.  AXN28D+ (Accentuate the positive)
10. AUYLOKS (Goldilocks; Au is the chemical symbol for gold)
11. DOC4JOX (Doc for jocks)
12. DRIBALZ (Doctor Eyeballs)
13. CALQL8R (Calculator)
14. CARPEPM (Carpe PM; play on Carpe Diem)
15. GDAYM8 (G'day, mate)
16. CTHRU U (See through you)
17. CRE8IV (Creative)
18. S5280FT (Smile; 5,280 feet = one mile)
19. IKNEADU (I knead you)
20. NYUKX3 (Nyuk! Nyuk! Nyuk!)

## BICYCLE AND WALKING WAITING GAMES (p. 58)

THAW WAIL SKY = WALK THIS WAY  ·  CARTWHEEL HORN SKIP = CHRISTOPHER WALKEN

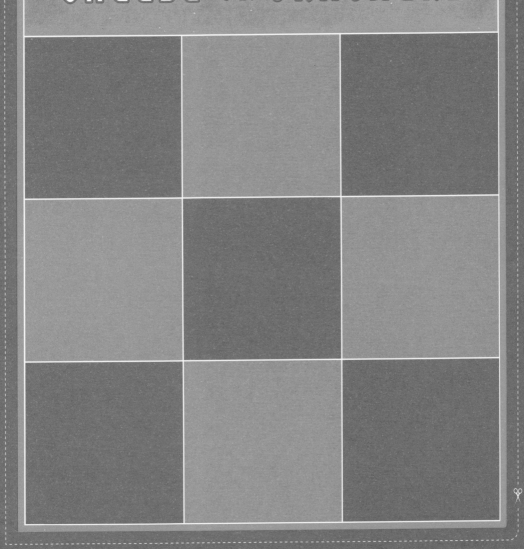

# CHEESE vs. CRACKERS

| B | I | N | G | O |
|---|---|---|---|---|
| 55 | WEIGH | 2 | LANE | LEFT |
| ONLY | SBARRO | SPEED | 65 | $1\frac{1}{2}$ |
| GAS | 45 | FREE SPACE | WAL-MART | WAY |
| 1 | FOOD | RIGHT | TOLL | 25 |
| MILES | YIELD | 70 | LIMIT | T.G.I. FRIDAY'S |

| B | I | N | G | O |
|---|---|---|---|---|
| LIMIT | TRUCKS | 2.5 | 45 | POLICE |
| WAY | GAS | 55 | McDON-ALD'S | NO |
| NEXT | 1 | FREE SPACE | TOLL | 35 |
| 65 | WAL-MART | MERGE | RIGHT | AMOCO |
| LEFT | 70 | CONGES-TION | BRIDGE | ONLY |

| B | I | N | G | O |
|---|---|---|---|---|
| DELAYS | RIGHT | 40 | 2 | TOLL |
| LEFT | BUS | MERGE | MILES | WAY |
| $1\frac{1}{4}$ | TRAFFIC | FREE SPACE | GAS | 65 |
| 35 | TACO BELL | BRIDGE | TRUCK | CONGES-TION |
| ONLY | SLOW | T.G.I. FRIDAY'S | 55 | EXIT |

| B | I | N | G | O |
|---|---|---|---|---|
| CONGES-TION | 1 | RAMP | RIGHT | WAL-MART |
| WAY | CHI-CHI'S | LEFT | BURGER KING | 65 |
| 2 | 40 | FREE SPACE | POLICE | MILES |
| BUS | TUNNEL | CARPOOL | 55 | EXXON |
| GAS | BUS | MERGE | TRAFFIC | SPEED |

And Don't Miss:

# COMPUTER WAITING GAMES

## THINGS TO DO WHILE DOWNLOADING, PROCESSING, OR CRASHING

by Hal Bowman

According to efficiency experts, the average computer user spends nine minutes every day waiting for files and web screens to download—that's more than 54 hours a year! With so much time a-wasting, you need *Computer Waiting Games*, a collection of how-to projects, puzzles, games, and activities to do while your computer toils away. Make a bird feeder out of floppy disks! Lose weight with Printer Cable Calisthenics! Play ten frames of Mouse Ball Bowling! And that's just the beginning—with a few basic supplies and a working computer, you can turn on-line frustration into plenty of rewarding creations. So what are you waiting for?

### LEARN HOW TO:

* Make a FREE TRIAL AOL CD Mobile
* Bench Press Your Computer Monitor
* Master Desk Chair Yoga
* Compose a Touch-Tone Telephone Symphony
* Harmonize Your Desktop with Feng Shui

ISBN 1-931686-02-5

$14.95

(price includes genuine mouse pad cover!)

Featuring Barbara as your Spokesmodel! ⟶